CW00662366

In additio
north dur
the north
generally
March da
the "craz

The patte
which he
quickly than sea. In summer, this produces an area
of low pressure over North Africa and Southern Asia,
which breaks up the belt of high pressure at about
30° north.

GLOBAL WINDS

Air tends to flow from high pressure to low pressure,
but its movement is deflected by the effect of the
Earth's rotation. In the northern hemisphere, moving
air masses tend to turn right: in the southern
hemisphere they tend to turn left. This is known as
the **Coriolis effect**, and produces a global pattern
of winds like this:

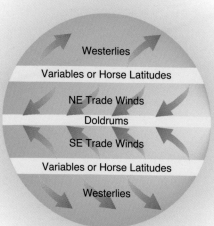

Westerlies

Variables or Horse Latitudes

NE Trade Winds

Doldrums

SE Trade Winds

Variables or Horse Latitudes

Westerlies

AIR MASSES

As it moves over land and sea, air takes on certain
characteristics: air which has flowed over a warm
sea, for instance, is warmer and wetter than air
which has flowed over a cold land-mass.

In the UK, these different types of air are often
given descriptive names:

Tropical Maritime	from SW = warm and wet
Polar Maritime	from NW = cool and moist
Polar Continental	from NE = cold and dry
Tropical Continental	from S or SE = dry and hot in summer, cool in winter

3. INTRODUCTION

WEATHER MAPS

Weather maps or synoptic charts are used to help us visualise the complex variations of temperature and pressure that affect our day-to-day wind and weather.

PRESSURE is shown by lines called isobars. Each isobar joins points that have the same atmospheric pressure, just as the contours on a navigational chart join points that are at the same height or depth.

Pressure is measured in millibars: normal atmospheric pressure is about 1000 mB ± 30 mB, and averages about 1013 mB.

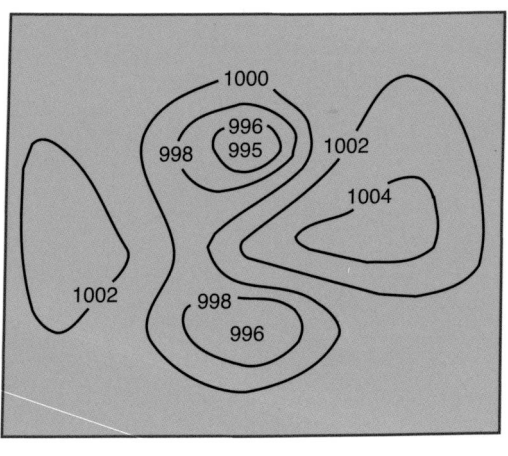

TEMPERATURE is not shown as such on the synoptic charts available to yachtsmen, but the boundaries between air masses at different temperatures are shown by lines called fronts.

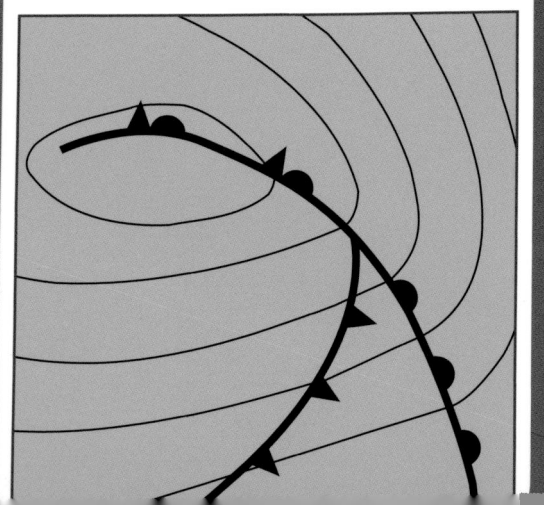

DEPRESSIONS (LOWS)

The weather around the UK is dominated by areas of low pressure called depressions, and their associated fronts. They grow out of distortions in the polar front which separates the warm tropical air south of about 50°N from the cooler polar air further north.

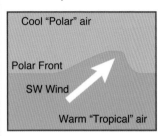

Cool "Polar" air

Polar Front

SW Wind

Warm "Tropical" air

Sometimes the southwesterly wind pushes a little pocket of warm air into the cooler air to the north.

The warm air is less dense than the cool air around it, so it creates a local area of low pressure. The surrounding air tries to fill the low, but is immediately affected by the Coriolis effect.

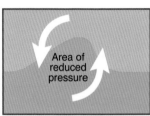

Area of reduced pressure

This sets up a swirling motion that exaggerates the original pocket of warm air.

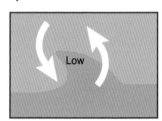

Low

In the northern hemisphere, the swirl is always anticlockwise. **Buys Ballot's Law** says: *"If you stand with your back to the wind, the centre of the depression is to your left".*

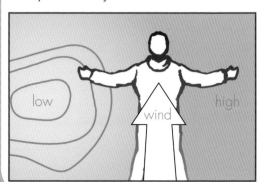

low

wind

WINDS AROUND DEPRESSIONS

On a weather map, a depression appears as a pattern of roughly concentric – and more or less circular – isobars.

About 500 m above the surface the wind blows very nearly parallel to the isobars. This is called the **geostrophic wind.** Using a hand bearing compass to measure the clouds' movement gives its direction.

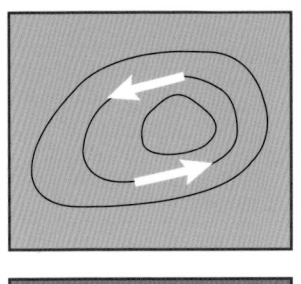

Over water, surface drag reduces the Coriolis effect, so the surface wind is angled inwards by about 10-20°.

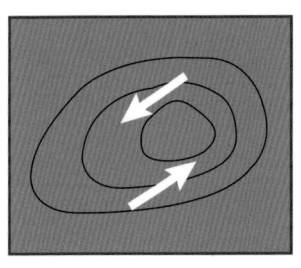

Over land, there is even more drag, so the surface wind is angled inwards by about 20-40°.

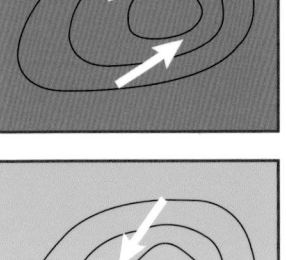

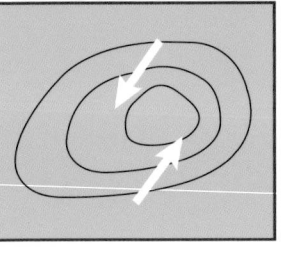

This helps depressions to fill more quickly over continental land-masses than over open ocean.

WIND STRENGTH is determined by the differences of pressure within the depression.

Where the pressure changes a lot in a short distance (shown by closely-spaced isobars) the winds will be strong. Where the isobars are far apart, winds will be light.

- In general, the surface wind over the sea is about 70% of the wind speed at 500 metres.

- Over land, it is more variable, but may be only about 50% of the wind speed at 500 metres.

A **front** is the word used to describe the leading edge of a moving air mass. A **warm front** is the front of a warm air mass, and a **cold front** is the front of a cold air mass, so as a depression passes to the north of you, you are likely to experience each in turn.

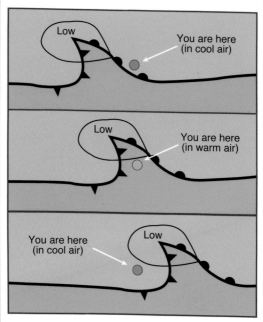

On a weather map, a warm front is usually marked with blobs, and a cold front is marked with spikes: the blobs or spikes point in the general direction in which the front is moving.

WHY FRONTS PRODUCE RAIN

When warm air catches up with cooler air (at a warm front) it slides upwards. At a cold front (where cool air catches up with warmer air) the cold air slides underneath, forcing the warm air upwards.

As the warm air rises, it expands and cools. Any moisture in the air condenses to form clouds and then drops of rain, hail, or snow.

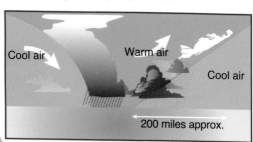

OCCLUDED FRONTS

Cold fronts generally move faster than warm fronts, so eventually the cold front will catch up with the warm front to form an occluded front (or occlusion). An occluded front may be described as "warm" or "cold" depending on the change of temperature as it passes, but both types generally produce cloud getting lower, then rain breaking up into showers.

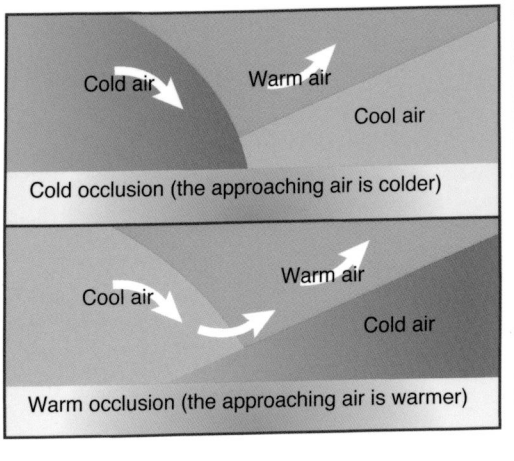

Cold occlusion (the approaching air is colder)

Warm occlusion (the approaching air is warmer)

ANTICYCLONES ("HIGHS")

Anticyclones, or areas of high pressure, are much less active features than depressions.

Their isobars are usually more widely spaced than those of a depression, so winds are generally light and the weather is generally fine, though in winter the sky may be overcast.

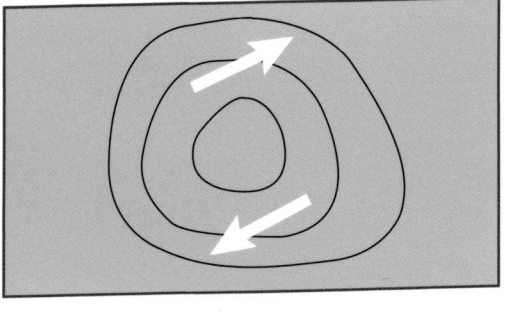

Once an anticyclone becomes established its movement is likely to be slow and irregular, and it may remain stationary for days or weeks on end.

The atmospheric stability associated with a high is likely to promote coastal fog in spring and autumn. In summer, trapped dust particles may form haze.

WEATHER AROUND DEPRESSIONS

The fronts associated with a typical depression divide the area around it into distinct sectors, each with distinctive weather patterns (see cover picture).

THE WARM FRONT
Wind	Increases and backs (e.g. from SW to S) as the front approaches, then veers (e.g. from SW to W) as the front passes
Cloud	Cloud cover increases and cloud base lowers as the front approaches
Weather	Rain, becoming heavier and continuous
Visibility	Reducing as the front approaches
Pressure	Falling as the front approaches

THE WARM SECTOR
(Between the fronts, generally S or SE of the depression's centre)
Wind	Steady
Cloud	Low cloud, almost 100% cover
Weather	Steady drizzle or light rain
Visibility	Moderate or poor, possibly foggy
Pressure	Steady

THE COLD FRONT
Wind	May increase and possibly back (e.g. from W to SW) as the front approaches, then veers (e.g. from W to NW) as the front passes
Cloud	Dense cloud, possibly towering to great heights at the front itself, quickly breaking up into to smaller puffy clouds once the front has passed
Weather	Heavy rain, followed by showers once the front has passed
Visibility	Poor in rain, then good or very good
Pressure	Rises as the front passes

THE COLD SECTOR
Wind	May veer a little and freshen or become gusty immediately behind the cold front (depending on the depth and movement of the depression)
Cloud	Apart from any frontal cloud nearby, generally clear skies with scattered showers or white 'fair weather cumulus'
Weather	Fair
Visibility	Generally good
Pressure	Depends on the depth and movement of the depression, but generally rises quickly as the cold front passes, then more slowly

PREDICTING WINDS FROM A SYNOPTIC CHART

Given a forecast synoptic chart, it is possible to predict the likely strength and direction of the wind in a given area by examining the isobars in the vicinity.

DIRECTION

To find the wind direction, measure the direction of the nearest isobars, bearing in mind that the wind blows so that the lowest pressure is on its left (see page 5).

In open water, subtract 10^0-20^0 from the direction of the isobars to find the direction of the surface wind.

Inland, subtract 20^0-40^0 from the direction of the isobars to find the direction of the surface wind.

STRENGTH

Measure the distance (in nautical miles) between the two nearest isobars, and use the table below to find the geostrophic wind strength (page 6).

Over sea, the surface wind speed is about two thirds of the geostrophic wind. Over land, it is about half the geostrophic wind.

Note that the table refers to isobars at 2 mb intervals. If your chart has isobars at 4 mb intervals, you should halve the measured distance (to reduce it to 2 mb intervals) before referring to the table.

		Latitude				
		40	**45**	**50**	**55**	**60**
Distance between isobars at 2 mb intervals (in nautical miles)	20	89	82	75	71	66
	30	60	55	50	47	44
	40	45	42	38	35	33
	50	36	33	30	28	26
	60	30	28	26	24	22
	70	26	25	23	21	19
	80	23	22	20	19	17
	90	20	19	17	16	15
	100	18	17	15	14	13
	120	15	14	13	12	11
	140	13	12	11	10	9
	160	11	10	9	9	8
	180	10	9	8	8	7
	200	8	8	7	7	6

PRODUCING YOUR OWN FORECAST CHART

Without a prepared forecast synoptic chart, any attempt at DIY forecasting for more than a few hours ahead needs to begin with the preparation of your own forecast synopsis. Obviously this is unlikely to be as accurate as one prepared by a professional meteorologist with high-tech resources at his disposal, but it can still be a valuable guide.

Ideally, you need to be able to visualise the swirling mass of the atmosphere – it may help if you can imagine the ripples and eddies created if you stir a basin of water – but there are a few general rules of thumb which can help.

DEPRESSIONS, around the UK and Europe, usually...

1. Move in an easterly or north-easterly direction, parallel to the line of the isobars in the warm sector.
2. If a depression has been moving in a particular direction for 12 hours, it is likely to go on doing so for another 12 hours unless it meets land or a large anticyclone.
3. Lows slow down and fill up when they meet land, or when their fronts occlude.
4. If the barometer is rising more quickly behind a depression than it fell when the depression approached, the depression is probably filling and slowing down (and vice versa).
5. When a large depression occludes, a smaller 'secondary' depression often develops somewhere along the trailing cold front.
6. If two similar lows are close to each other they may merge to form a complex low, with two centres that rotate anticlockwise around each other.

FRONTS

1. Each section of a front moves at right angles to the line representing the front itself.
2. Each section of a cold front moves at about the speed of the geostrophic wind behind it. Warm fronts typically move about 30% slower.

LAND AND SEA BREEZES

The temperature of the sea surface changes only slowly. By comparison, the temperature of the land may change quickly and dramatically between night and day. As the land warms up, the air above it also warms and rises, leaving a local area of low pressure. Cool air from the sea flows in to fill the low, setting up an onshore **SEA BREEZE**.

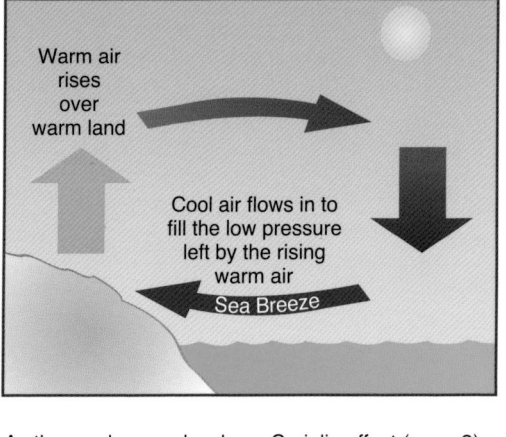

Warm air rises over warm land

Cool air flows in to fill the low pressure left by the rising warm air

Sea Breeze

As the sea breeze develops, Coriolis effect (page 3) may become significant, making the sea breeze veer (swing to the right) by 60^0-70^0 until it is almost parallel to the shore.

Sea breezes are most noticeable:
* In summer, especially when clear skies allow the direct rays of the sun to heat the land quickly during the day.
* In the afternoon, when the land has had time to warm up to its maximum temperature.

Sea breezes can reach 20 knots at the coast, and some effect may be felt 10-20 miles offshore.

Small islands (such as Alderney or the Isle of Wight) are not big enough to sustain a sea breeze for long: as soon as the sea breeze starts, it cools the island and kills the sea breeze.

LAND BREEZES are opposite in direction to sea breezes, and are caused by the land cooling at night. This cools the air over the land, which becomes denser and therefore drains downwards towards the sea. Land breezes are generally lighter than sea breezes, and are not felt as far offshore. But extreme versions of this effect can be felt in mountainous regions, where the offshore wind can reach gale force. In such conditions this 'drainage wind' is known as a **Katabatic wind**.

COASTAL EFFECTS

Whenever air flows over the surface of the Earth, drag reduces the speed of the surface wind to less than that of the geostrophic wind at an altitude of a few hundred metres.

At sea, this produces a surface wind which is angled about 10-20^0 anticlockwise from the geostrophic wind. Over land, the effect is more pronounced, and the surface wind is angled about 20-40^0 anticlockwise from the geostrophic wind. This means the wind direction over the sea differs by about 20-30^0 from that over the land.

Where the wind is blowing generally offshore, it makes this 'alteration of course' gradually, in a zone extending up to about 5 miles offshore.

Where the wind is generally onshore, a similar effect occurs a few miles inland.

CONVERGENCE AND DIVERGENCE
When the wind is blowing along the coast, the difference in wind directions over land and sea has a different effect.

If the land is to your right when you are standing with your back to the wind (i.e. if the low pressure is to seaward of the coast) the winds over the land and sea will be converging with each other, creating a funnelling effect: the wind along the coast will be stronger than offshore.

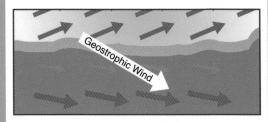

If the land is to your left when you are standing with your back to the wind (i.e. if the low pressure is to landward of the coast) the winds over the land and sea will be diverging from each other so the coastal wind will be lighter than offshore.

RAIN AND CLOUD

In general, air temperature decreases with height – typically at about 0.5 °C per 100 metres. This is known as the lapse rate.

When air near sea level becomes warmer than the air above it, it tends to rise. As a 'bubble' of air rises, it moves into progressively reducing pressure, so it expands. As it expands, it gets cooler, at a rate of about 1 °C per 100 metres, until it reaches a level at which it is the same temperature as the air around it.

If the temperature of the surrounding air is reducing more quickly than the bubble temperature, the bubble of air will continue to rise: this produces conditions described as **'unstable'**.

If the temperature of the surrounding air is reducing more slowly than usual, the bubble of air will not be able to rise as far or as quickly: this produces **'stable'** conditions.

In some situations, the air a few hundred metres above the surface may be warmer than that at ground level: this produces an extreme form of stability known as an **inversion**.

PRECIPITATION

Precipitation is a generic word for drizzle, rain, hail, snow or sleet, and is likely whenever moist air is cooled, e.g.:

* by passing over a cool surface
* by being forced upwards over high ground
* by rising over cooler air (e.g. at a front)

When air is warm, it can hold a considerable amount of invisible water vapour. As it cools, the water vapour condenses to form water droplets or ice crystals. These produce cloud or fog (fog is effectively just cloud which has formed at surface level).

If the air is cooled still further, the water droplets eventually merge together to form drops which are too heavy to be supported by the rising air and which therefore fall as **rain** or **hail**.

If the air is fairly dry, the water vapour will not condense until it reaches temperatures below freezing point. If this happens at ground level, the condensing water immediately forms ice crystals called frost. If it happens in low clouds, the ice crystals clump together to form **snow**.

TYPES OF CLOUD

Meteorologists classify clouds mainly by their height and shape, and often combine two descriptive terms into a complex name such as cirrostratus or stratocumulus.

HEIGHT
High cloud (cloud base between 6 and 12 km) is called cirrus or is given the prefix **cirro-**.

Medium cloud (cloud base between 2 and 6 km) is given the prefix **alto-**.

Low cloud is usually classified by its shape, with no special prefix.

SHAPE
Clouds which are generally flat are described as stratus or are given the prefix **strato-**.

Clouds which are towering or puffy are described as **cumulus** or are given the prefix **cumulo-**.

OTHER WORDS
Rain-producing clouds are described as **nimbus** or given the prefix **nimbo-**.

Clouds which appear to have been broken up by wind are given the prefix **fracto-**.

Cirrus: very high wispy clouds formed of ice crystals.

Cirrostratus: high sheets of thin ice cloud, often producing a halo effect around the sun or moon.

16. CLOUDS & RAIN

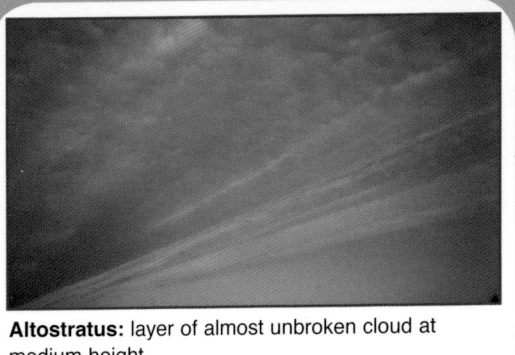

Altostratus: layer of almost unbroken cloud at medium height.

Altocumulus: fairly high 'woolly' looking cloud.

Stratus: almost continuous sheets of low cloud; often grey and associated with drizzle.

Cumulus: low, puffy clouds. Sometimes white and associated with fair weather but may grow upwards, produce showers and take on some of

Cumulonimbus: the classic 'thundercloud', with a fairly low cloud base but very high top (often flat): it may be up to 4-5 km from top to bottom. Its great height is caused by rising air currents inside the cloud, which allow large raindrops or hail to develop.

Nimbostratus: low, heavy looking sheets of grey cloud, associated with continuous rain (e.g. at a warm front).

Fractostratus: very low, ragged clouds associated with wet and windy weather.

Stratocumulus: an apparently contradictory name applied to cumulus clouds that have spread out and combined to form a broken sheet, or to thin stratus that appears to be breaking up into separate clouds.

17. CLOUDS & RAIN

FOG

Fog is formed when moist air near the surface is cooled sufficiently for its water vapour to condense into water droplets. The process is identical to that which creates clouds.

Hill fog is formed when moist air moves inland and rises over high ground, cooling and condensing as it goes.

Radiation fog is formed over land on clear, quiet nights, when the land cools quickly, radiating its heat into space. This, in turn, cools the air in contact with the land, allowing its water vapour to condense into fog, which may drift out to sea. It is common in coastal waters in winter and spring, especially near large towns, but generally clears during the morning and seldom extends more than a few miles offshore.

Advection fog or **sea fog** is formed when warm moist air flows over a colder sea surface which cools the lower layers of the air. It is particularly associated with cold ocean currents, but around the UK it is common in winter and spring, when the sea is at its coldest. Sea fog may last for days on end, and is not 'blown away' by wind: on the contrary, a SW wind may feed the fog by providing a continuous supply of moist air.

Frontal fog may form along a warm front or occlusion, especially if the air ahead of the front is very cold. It is caused by the warm air mixing with or being cooled by the colder air ahead of it, so it is very limited in extent, but may give way to sea fog in the warm sector.

Arctic sea smoke, despite its name, is not confined to the Arctic! It is formed when cold air flows over a relatively warm sea. As it does so, the air in contact with the sea is warmed up and absorbs moisture. As it warms, it rises, and is immediately cooled by the cold air above. The process is very similar to that which goes on above a mug of hot tea! Around the UK it is rare at sea, but is quite common over rivers and estuaries on frosty winter mornings.

THUNDERSTORMS AND SQUALLS

Thunderstorms may be generated along active cold fronts or over land on still, hot summer days. In both cases, strong convection currents are set up, and build large cumulonimbus clouds.

Raindrops in these large clouds grow so big that they disintegrate. This creates a charge of static electricity – which is eventually discharged to produce lightning and thunder.

Lightning is attracted to high points (such as a yacht's mast), but is usually discharged quickly and safely through the mast and rigging to the sea. Very strong and rapidly shifting winds can be expected just in front of a thundercloud, as the cloud effectively 'sucks' air in from around it. Squalls generally pose a greater threat to small craft than the risk of lightning.

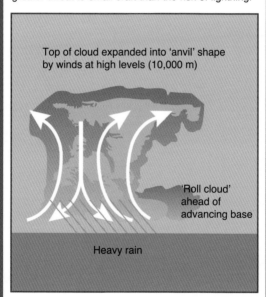

Top of cloud expanded into 'anvil' shape by winds at high levels (10,000 m)

'Roll cloud' ahead of advancing base

Heavy rain

LINE SQUALLS

Line squalls may occur along the line of very active cold fronts, particularly if there is a marked kink in the isobars (i.e. shift in wind direction) along the line of the front. They are marked by a clearly-defined black 'roll cloud', similar to that at the leading edge of a thunderstorm. The effect is similar: strong gusts of wind followed by heavy rain, but in extreme cases the turbulence may be enough to trigger waterspouts or tornadoes, representing a real danger to small craft that is best avoided by aiming to pass under the lightest part of the approaching roll cloud.

METEOROLOGICAL TERMINOLOGY

To simplify the description of weather, meteorologists use very specific terminology.

WIND STRENGTH: THE BEAUFORT SCALE

	wind speed (kts)	descriptive term	sea state in open water and max. wave height (in m)	
0	<1	calm	mirror-like	
1	1-3	light air	ripples	0.1
2	4-6	light breeze	small wavelets	0.3
3	7-10	gentle breeze	some breaking crests	1
4	11-16	moderate breeze	fairly frequent white horses	1.5
5	17-21	fresh breeze	many white horses, and possibly some spray	2.5
6	22-27	strong breeze	extensive white horses and spray	4
7	28-33	near gale	foam begins to form streaks downwind from crests	5.5
8	34-40	gale	well-marked foam streaks	7.5
9	41-47	severe gale	tumbling crests, spray may affect visibility	10
10	48-55	storm	sea surface generally white with foam	12.5
11	56-63	violent storm	wave crests blown into froth, forming long white patches on surface	16
12	>64	hurricane	air filled with foam and spray, surface white, visibility badly affected	>16

The wind speeds refer to sustained wind speed (at 10 m above the surface), not to transient gusts which may be considerably stronger.

Note that the sea state descriptions are a guide to what may be expected in the open sea: the Beaufort scale should not be used to describe sea states, and you should bear in mind that conditions may be very

SEA STATE

code	descriptive term	wave height (m)*
0	calm – glassy	0
1	calm – rippled	0-0.1
2	smooth	0.1-0.5
3	slight	0.5-1.25
4	moderate	1.25-2.5
5	rough	2.5-4.0
6	very rough	4-6
7	high	6-9
8	very high	9-14
9	phenomenal	>14

*crest to trough

VISIBILITY

Different terms are used to describe visibility, depending on the context – land, sea, or air.

	marine	aviation & coastal	land
> 5 NM	good		
2-5 NM	moderate		
1km-2NM	poor		
1km-2km		mist or haze	
200m-1km			fog
50m-200m	fog	fog	thick fog
<50m			dense fog

TIMING

Timing can be crucial, especially if you are looking for a 'weather window' in which to make a dash for home.

	time from issue of forecast
imminent	<6 hours
soon	6-12 hours
later	>12 hours

MOVEMENT OF WEATHER SYSTEMS

slowly	<15 knots
steadily	15-25 knots
rather quickly	25-35 knots
rapidly	35-45 knots
very rapidly	>45 knots

PRESSURE CHANGES

	change in past 3 hours
steady	>0.1 mb
slowly	0.1-1.5 mb
rising or falling	1.6-3.5 mb
quickly	3.6-6.0 mb
very rapidly	>6.0 mb
now rising now falling	a previous trend has reversed, and pressure is NOW rising or NOW falling.

21. TERMINOLOGY

USEFUL SYMBOLS AND ABBREVIATIONS

THE BEAUFORT NOTATION

clear sky	b	overcast	o
partly cloudy	bc	showers	p
cloudy	c	squall	q
drizzle	d	rain	r
fog	f	sleet	rs
gale	g	snow	s
hail	h	thunder	t
lightning	l	thunderstorm	tl / tlr
mist	m	haze	z

Capital letters suggest 'heavy'. **Repeated letters** suggest 'continuous'. A **slash** suggests the passage of time. E.g. **RR/pr** suggests "continuous heavy rain then rain showers".

WIND ARROWS

Wind 'arrows' may be used on weather charts to show the wind strength and direction. The direction is shown by the direction the arrow is pointing, and the strength by the number of 'feathers' on its tail. Each full feather represents two forces on the Beaufort scale.

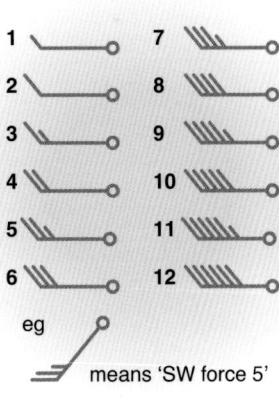

means 'SW force 5'

ADDING STATION REPORTS TO A SYNOPSIS

When drawing your own weather map from a general synopsis and station reports, it is important to appreciate the passage of time. For instance, the Shipping Forecast you hear being broadcast at 0048 will have been issued at 2300, and based on a synoptic chart drawn up from weather reports gathered at 1900. New reports will be coming in while the forecast is being prepared, so the Coastal Station Reports at the end of the Shipping Forecast will be information gathered at 2200.

synopsis time	coastal reports	issued at	broadcast
1900	2200	2300	0048
0100	0400	0500	0520
0700	1000	1100	1201
1300	1600	1700	1754